Customs Around the World

SHOPPING
Around the World

by Wil Mara

PEBBLE
a capstone imprint

T0084504

Pebble Explore is published by Pebble, an imprint of Capstone.
1710 Roe Crest Drive
North Mankato, Minnesota 56003
www.capstonepub.com

**Library of Congress Cataloging-in-Publication Data is available on
the Library of Congress website.**
ISBN: 978-1-9771-2375-6 (hardcover)
ISBN: 978-1-9771-2675-7 (paperback)
ISBN: 978-1-9771-2412-8 (eBook PDF)

Summary: Go on a global shopping trip! Look for clothes in a mall.
Buy fresh food at an outdoor market. Discover how people around the
world shop in this engaging series that develops kids' understanding
of our diverse global community and their place in it.

Image Credits
AFP via Getty Images: SIMON MAINA / Contributor, 16; Alamy: MARKA,
21, Shopping/Peter Forsberg, 17, Terry Harris, 22; Shutterstock: Aran
Chalermsaen, Cover, bonandbon, 10, Colin Hui, 9, Ekaphon maneechot, 28,
ESB Professional, 27, Iakov Filimonov, 5, Jess Kraft, 25, John Wollwerth,
26, Marco Fine, 13, Marija Vujosevic, 23, Monkey Business Images, 1,
pang_oasis, 19, photo.ua, 15, Prostock-studio, 8, S-F, 11, Shang Li, 20,
Spectral-Design, 7, topten22photo, 18

Design Elements
Capstone; Shutterstock: Stawek (map), VLADGRIN

Editorial Credits
Editor: Abby Huff; Designer: Julie Peters; Media Researcher: Jo Miller;
Production Specialist: Spencer Rosio

Consultant Credits
Bryan K. Miller, PhD
Research Affiliate of Museum of Anthropological Archaeology
University of Michigan

All internet sites appearing in back matter were available and accurate
when this book was sent to press.

Printed in the United States
PO117

TABLE OF CONTENTS

Words in **bold** are in the glossary.

LET'S TAKE A SHOPPING TRIP

Everybody shops. We buy things we need. We shop for food and clothes. But we also buy things we want, such as books and games. Some people even shop for fun!

Around the world, there are many shopping **customs**. People shop in different ways. Some like to visit stores. Others stay home and do their shopping **online**. What does your shopping trip look like?

WAYS TO SHOP

How do you shop? Many people go out to buy things. They see **goods** in person. In some countries, people visit shopping streets. These have lots of stores. In Argentina, cars cannot drive on Florida Street. This is so people can easily walk to the shops.

Other areas are known for selling certain things. For example, shops in Paris, France, are known for having nice clothing. Shoppers can buy the latest fashions.

People shopping on Florida Street

Another way to shop is online. People can search for many kinds of goods. The goods will be shipped right to the person's door.

Online shopping is very popular in the United Kingdom. Many people buy clothes and shoes. Most shop on Sundays.

Shopping online in China

In China, people do a lot of shopping on their phones. They can read online what other buyers liked. It helps people decide what to buy.

BIG PLACES, LITTLE PLACES

Some shopping places are very big. Malls are large buildings with many stores and places to eat inside. People may spend an entire day at a mall.

The United States is famous for its malls. The first one was built in 1956. Today there are more than 1,000.

The outside of a U.S. mall

The Dubai Mall in the
United Arab Emirates

One of the biggest malls is in the
United Arab Emirates. It has 1,200
stores. It even has an ice rink! More
than 80 million people visit each year.

Are you in a hurry? Try shopping at a small place. A popular choice in many countries is **convenience stores**. They are often open long hours. They sell snacks, newspapers, and other things people may need quickly.

Many convenience stores in Japan are open day and night. They're known for having fresh meals. People like to get the meals when they don't have time to cook.

GOING TO THE MARKET

People all over the world shop at **markets**. These have many sellers in the same place. Sellers often have goods they have made, such as clothing or furniture. They might also sell things they have grown, like fruits and vegetables.

Inside the Grand Bazaar

One of the oldest and biggest markets is in Turkey. It is called the Grand Bazaar. It has more than 4,000 shops. They are all inside a building. This is called a covered market.

Other markets are outdoors. In Kenya, some sellers in **Maasai** markets set out their goods under tents. But others don't use any covers. They put their goods on blankets on the ground. Maasai markets are often set up in different places during the week.

A Maasai market

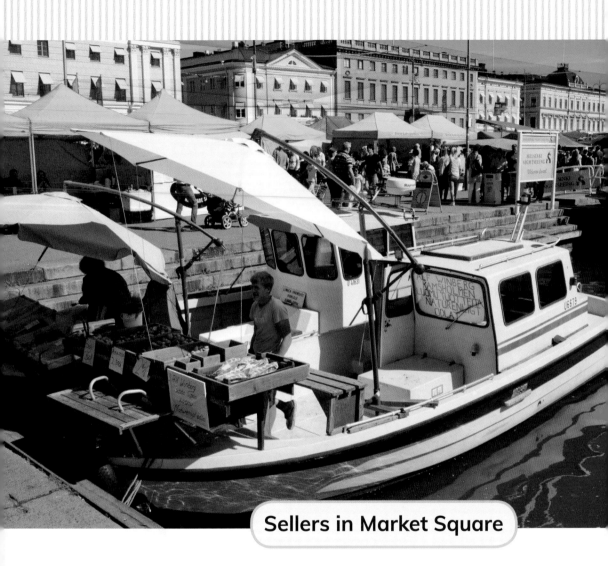

Sellers in Market Square

In Finland, the Market Square is set up near the water. Some people sell fresh fish right from their boat.

Markets can be set up in many ways. Floating markets are common in Thailand. People sell goods from small boats on the river. Shoppers are also taken by boats to visit them.

Shopping on a river in Thailand

A night market in Laos

    In Laos, some markets only appear at night. Sellers set up their tents after it gets dark. They take them down before midnight. And in Canada, Christmas markets happen only during the holiday season. People can buy a hot chocolate to drink while they shop.

GETTING GROCERIES

Feeling hungry? Then it's time to buy food. In Australia, people often make one or two trips each week to get **groceries**. Many go to a supermarket. These are big stores that sell food. They also sell everyday things such as toilet paper or cleaning supplies.

A supermarket in Australia

Supermarket shoppers in Italy put on gloves to pick up fruits and vegetables. This is so they don't touch food they are not buying.

In other places, people buy food almost every day. People in Greece may visit many shops. They go to a butcher shop for meat. Then they go to a bakery for bread.

A Greek bakery

A fruit stand in Cuba

Fresh food is important in some **cultures**. In Cuba, farmers often set up stands. They sell fruit and vegetables they have grown. In South Korea, many people like seafood. So they may go to fish markets. They buy fish that was caught the same day.

PAYING

How much will you pay for the things you want? In some places, you can **bargain**. This is when a seller asks for one price. The buyer wants to pay less. They talk and try to agree on a new price.

Shoppers in Tunisia need to bargain. Many sellers at markets set their prices high. They expect buyers will ask for lower prices.

Bargaining in Tunisia

You're ready to buy. How do you pay? One way is to use **cash**. This includes coins and paper bills. Most countries have their own kind of money. In Ethiopia, people pay for most things with cash. Their money is called the *birr*.

Paying with birr in Ethiopia

Other people don't carry cash. They may use **credit cards** or their phones to pay. In Sweden, some stores don't even take cash anymore!

There are many shopping choices. You can visit a store or mall. You can go to a market. You can buy online. Things will be shipped right to you. How will you be shopping in the years ahead?

MAP

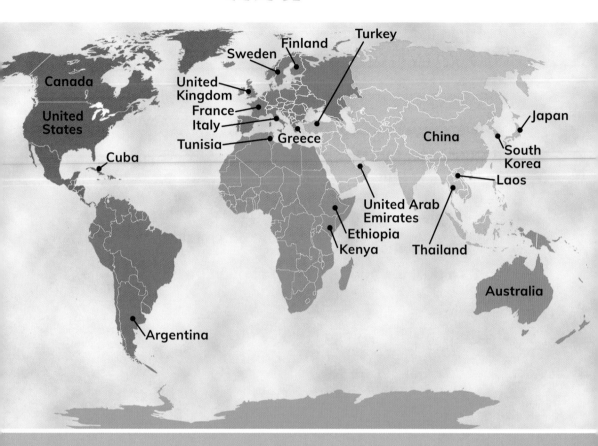

Canada

United States

Cuba

Argentina

United Kingdom

France

Italy

Tunisia

Sweden

Finland

Greece

Turkey

United Arab Emirates

Ethiopia

Kenya

China

Thailand

Japan

South Korea

Laos

Australia

Around the world, people shop in different ways. See which places were talked about in this book!

GLOSSARY

bargain (BAHR-guhn)—to talk over the price of an item and try to come to an agreement

cash (KASH)—money such as coins and bills

convenience store (kuhn-VEEN-yuns STOHR)—a small store that is often open long hours and sells basic items

credit card (KREH-dit KARD)—a plastic card that lets a person buy something and pay for it later

culture (KUHL-chur)—a group of people's beliefs and way of life

custom (KUHS-tuhm)—a usual way of doing something in a place or for a group of people

goods (GUDZ)—things that can be bought or sold

groceries (GROH-sur-eez)—food bought from a store

Maasai (MAH-sigh)—a group of people in Kenya who are traveling animal herders

market (MAHR-kit)—a place where people gather to sell and buy items

online (on-LINE)—done over the internet, a system that connects computers all over the world

READ MORE

Johnson, Robin. *Art in Different Places*. New York, Crabtree Publishing Company, 2017.

Meinking, Mary. *Our Farmers' Market*. North Mankato, MN: Pebble, 2020.

Reina, Mary. *Spend Money*. North Mankato, MN: Pebble, 2020.

INTERNET SITES

10 Great Traditional Markets Around the World
www.momondo.com/discover/article/10-great-traditional-markets-around-the-world

Globe Trottin' Kids
www.globetrottinkids.com

What a Week of Groceries Looks Like Around the World
fstoppers.com/food/what-week-groceries-looks-around-world-3251

INDEX